D0296618

SIKHS
IN BRITAIN

Fiona Macdonald

Consultant: Rajinder Singh Panesar

Photography by Chris Fairclough

FRANKLIN WATTS
LONDON • SYDNEY

First published in 2005 by
Franklin Watts
96 Leonard Street
London
EC2A 4XD

Franklin Watts Australia
Level 17/207 Kent Street
Sydney NSW 2000

Copyright © 2005 Franklin Watts

A CIP catalogue record for this book
is available from the British Library
Dewey number 305.6'946'041

Planning and production by
Discovery Books Limited
Editors: Kate Taylor and Laura Durman
Designer: Rob Norridge

The author, packager and publisher would like to thank the following people
for their participation in this book: The Deogan family, Bhai Sahib Bhai
Mohinder Singh Ji, Wilkes Green Junior School, Mr A.S. Mangat MBE BSc,
Onkar Eye Centre & Mr G. S. Changan BSc (hons) M C Optom., DTF Book
Shop, Soho Supermarket, Badial.

Photo acknowledgements: All by Chris Fairclough besides:
P6 Topical Press Agency/Getty Images; P7, Thurston Hopkins/Picture
Post/Getty Images; P26 top, AFP/Getty Images

ISBN: 0 7496 5883 5

Printed in Dubai

Contents

British and Sikh

Around 336,000 Sikhs live in Britain today. They are one of the nation's smallest minority groups – just 0.6 per cent of the total population.

Sikh men and women play a prominent part in British life. There are Sikh politicians, doctors, lawyers, professors, business leaders, artists and media stars in Britain. All follow a faith that encourages them to take action – for their country, their family and their community.

Young and old members of the Sikh community in Birmingham wait to watch a festival procession pass by.

Multicultural society

Traditionally, Sikhism promotes tolerance, justice and respect for all religions. Sikh people were some of the first in Britain to stand up for their rights and challenge old rules and prejudices about race and religion. At times, this led to conflict, suspicion and controversy.

Punjab

Unlike many other British faith communities, most Sikhs share the same ethnic heritage, as well as the same religion. Their ancestors originated in Punjab, now divided between India and Pakistan. They may speak Punjabi, as well as English and perhaps Hindi (India's official language) or Urdu (the main language of Pakistan). Sikhs often observe many customs and traditions originating from the Punjab region.

British identity

Because of this strong cultural and ethnic identity, some Sikh leaders in Britain are calling for their community to be given its own special status and protection by the Race Relations Act. At the same time, a recent survey showed that the vast majority of Sikhs were proud of their British identity.

A father helps his daughter choose a book at a shop selling Urdu and Punjabi publications.

> I am fiercely loyal as an officer with the West Midlands Police but I am equally at home with my faith. They are in perfect harmony.

PC Harvinder Singh Rai.

Arriving and settling

Sikhs first arrived in Britain during the 18th century. They travelled as servants, bodyguards and clerks to the British merchants trading with India.

The earliest recorded Sikh to settle permanently was Maharajah Duleep Singh, last king of Punjab. The Maharajah (aged 14) was removed from his throne in 1849 by British troops, to punish Sikh warriors who had been fighting them. He was brought to Britain, where he lived in a stylish stately home and became friends with Queen Victoria.

Soldiers

Many more Sikhs came to live in Britain from the early 20th century. The first Sikh gurdwara (temple) in London was founded in 1911. Some early settlers were traders and scholars, but most were soldiers. Over 100,000 Sikh troops fought with skill and bravery on the British side during World War I (1914-1918). Sikhs also served with distinction in Britain's later wars.

Lieutenant Panai Singh, an officer in the British army, photographed with his horse in London in 1918.

Emigration

The 1950s and 1960s were peak years for Sikh emigration to Britain. Then, Sikhs – mostly from poor, uneducated farming families – left their homes in Punjab to find work and escape fighting, following civil unrest between India and Pakistan. There was more violence in Punjab in 1966, and thousands of Sikh homes and farms were destroyed. Immigrants found low-paid jobs in factories in London, Birmingham and West Yorkshire. These districts are still home to Britain's largest Sikh communities today.

Young Sikh children, newly arrived in Britain in 1955. The boys wear English-style short trousers but have tied up their long hair in traditional topknots and turbans.

East Africa

In the 1960s and 1970s, Sikhs from East Africa (who had emigrated there from India long before) were driven out by governments of newly independent nations: Kenya, Tanzania and Uganda. Many belonged to wealthy, educated families. Unlike earlier Sikh settlers, they came to Britain and found work in well-paid, respected professions.

INDIA AND PAKISTAN

In 1947, the Indian subcontinent was divided into two newly-independent nations, India (mostly Hindu) and Pakistan (mostly Muslim). Since 1947, the people and governments of India and Pakistan have fought or argued continuously about their borders. Kashmir and Punjab are two of the territories that have been disputed since the split in 1947. Millions of Hindus, Sikhs and Muslims have become refugees or been killed in fighting between the two states.

The Sikh faith

Sikhism is one of the world's youngest faiths, originating in the Punjab nearly 500 years ago. It was first taught by Guru Nanak, a spiritual leader who lived from 1469–1539. At that time, most Indians were Hindus, but many of their rulers were Muslims and there were quarrels between the two faiths.

Guru Nanak

Guru Nanak believed that there was only one God, the Creator of the world. He said that God did not belong to any one faith, and could be worshipped in many different ways. He called for tolerance and social equality, and asked his followers to be hard working, honest and generous, and to care for others.

THE KHANDA

The Khanda is the Sikh religious symbol. It appears on the Nishan Sahib – a triangular orange flag flown outside every gurdwara. It contains three separate parts. In the centre, a sword represents Divine Knowledge, with sharp edges to separate truth from falsehood. The circle surrounding it, called Chakkar, represents the perfection of God. The two curved swords on the outside represent Miri (duty in this world) and Piri (spiritual duty).

The ten Gurus who founded the Sikh religion.

Freedom from suffering

Guru Nanak believed in reincarnation (that people die and are reborn), according to the law of Karma (consequences of past actions). With God's help, he believed they could learn to lead better lives each time they were reincarnated, and would eventually join God and find eternal 'Mukti' (freedom from suffering).

At a gurdwara, the Guru Granth Sahib is honoured like a living holy man. It is seated on a silk cushion, and the reader waves a traditional Chauri (a special fan) in front of it.

The Guru Granth Sahib

After Guru Nanak died, his teachings were passed on to nine further Gurus. The tenth, Guru Gobind Singh (lived 1675–1708), was the last human Guru. He told Sikhs that in future they must be guided by scriptures (teachings, poems, hymns and prayers) known as the Guru Granth Sahib, and that these should be treated as the eleventh, and last, Guru. Today, these are kept in a place of honour in each gurdwara, and treated with great reverence.

Living as a Sikh

Sikhs follow their faith in two different ways: by worshipping God, and by helping the community. Sewa (service to others) is an essential part of Sikh life, together with giving to charity. In Britain, the Queen honours many Sikhs every year for 'services to the community'.

Worship

Sikhs worship at home by saying prayers, reading holy books or meditating. They also join public worship at a gurdwara. About 40 per cent of British Sikhs attend regularly; others visit at religious festivals, or for weddings and funerals. Prayers are held at gurdwaras every day, but many Sikhs visit once a week, on Sunday, when they have time off work. To show respect, they cover their heads, remove their shoes and wash their hands and feet before entering the prayer-hall.

Sikh men and women worship together in a gurdwara in Southall, London. Their heads are covered, and they have removed their shoes.

> My religion guides me in everyday life. Everything I do is a result of my faith and I am proud to be a Sikh. I am also proud to be British and feel strongly about trying to help in my community.

Sikh student, London.

Gurdwaras

There are around 200 gurdwaras in Britain. Some are large and splendid, others are small and simple. The walls may be decorated with pictures of Gurus or scenes from Sikh history (none contain pictures of God). All gurdwaras have a room for worship, where the Guru Granth Sahib is displayed under a canopy during the day, and a smaller room, where it is carefully stored at night.

There is also a kitchen, the langar, where volunteers prepare food for visitors. The food is vegetarian as most Sikhs do not eat meat. The food is served to anyone who wants it, and is available 24 hours a day. Kitchen helpers also prepare karah parshad – a mixture of wheat, sugar and butter, shared among worshippers as a sign of God's generosity. Sometimes, dried fruit and nuts are handed around, instead.

Children learning the Punjabi language and traditional Punjabi culture at a gurdwara school.

Providing for the community

The gurdwara also provides warm clothes for needy people, and a safe place to shelter, together with information, help and advice. Mother and baby groups, clubs for elderly people, and classes in traditional Punjabi culture are also held at gurdwaras.

The Khalsa

Sikh men and women who feel deeply committed to their religion choose to join the Khalsa Panth (brotherhood). This is a fellowship founded in 1699 by Guru Gobind Singh. Its purpose is to unite Sikh believers and strengthen them in their faith.

Khalsa

Guru Gobind Singh taught Khalsa members that they must live according to key Sikh principles of justice, tolerance and belief in one God. In addition, they must wear five physical signs of their faith. These are the Panj Kakke, often called 'the five Ks'.

A boy is initiated into the Khalsa. From now on he will add Singh to his surname.

Singh and Kaur

To emphasise their equality, Guru Gobind Singh gave Khalsa members new surnames, to replace old family names that revealed their social status. Men were called 'Singh' (Lion) and women 'Kaur' (Princess) – today, Sikhs often use these names alongside their old surnames. Guru Gobind Singh reminded the Khalsa to defend the Sikh faith and to help oppressed people.

Initiation

Today, men and women are initiated into the Khalsa during a ceremony in a gurdwara, in front of the Guru Granth Sahib. They drink amrit (sugar and water, stirred with a Sikh sword as a blessing) and sprinkle it on their eyes and hair. Once the ceremony is over, and from then on, they are called 'Amritdhari'.

PANJ KAKKE – THE FIVE KS

Kesh – uncut hair, for men and women. A sign of respect for God's Creation, and to be close to nature. Sikh men, and some women, wear a turban, to cover their long hair.

Kangha – a comb to keep hair neat and tidy. A symbol of self control.

Kachera – shorts. Traditionally, worn by warriors. A sign of purity and modesty.

Kara – a steel bangle. A sign of God's unity.

Kirpan – a sword. A sign that the Khalsa should defend the Sikh faith and protect the weak.

Devotion

As a sign of purity, Khalsa Sikhs get up very early to wash all over and put on clean clothes. Both are signs of spiritual purity. They meditate and say special prayers morning, evening and night. Many Sikhs who are not members of the Khalsa also pray, meditate, wear the 'five Ks' and put on turbans.

Turbans

A turban is a proud symbol of Sikh identity, a public sign of loyalty, and a constant reminder of the Gurus' teachings. In 1976, a new law in Britain made it compulsory for everyone to wear crash-helmets when riding motorcycles. Sikhs protested, demanding the right to continue wearing turbans, instead. In 1978, the British government finally agreed.

Turbans are made from a long, narrow piece of cloth, wound round the head many times. It takes skill and practice to tie them neatly.

> **The Turban Victory is truly a victory in many ways. It is a victory for the cause of individual and religious freedom; it is a victory for the Sikh community in confirming its identity...**
>
> *Siri Singh Sahib Harbhajan Singh Khalsa Yogiji, London, 1978.*

A Sikh home

Eight out of every ten Sikh families in Britain own their homes. The average Sikh family contains 3.6 people (compared with the national average of 2.2). Close relatives, such as grandparents, parents and grandchildren, or married brothers and their families, often share the same house. Only 13 per cent of Sikh people live alone.

Three generations of a Sikh family smile for the camera in the garden of their home.

"I have wonderful memories of playing cricket and rounders in the park. It was a real family affair – with more than enough cousins, aunts and uncles to make up opposing teams. Sometimes we would have 30 or 40 people around the table for a meal afterwards.

Amrit Kaur Singh, north-west England.

Welcoming

There is a strong Sikh tradition of providing food to needy strangers, and of welcoming friends and relatives to share meals. Women are usually responsible for the cooking, although some younger Sikh men help with household chores.

Cooking spicy curry. Many older Sikh people in Britain prefer Punjabi-style foods. But younger British Sikhs often enjoy dishes from many different lands.

A tray of Punjabi food — including chapatti (flat bread), pickles, yoghurt, fresh vegetables and rice — prepared at the langar (kitchen) of a gurdwara.

Food

Sikhs in Britain often like to eat traditional Punjabi foods, such as aloo mattar (spiced potatoes and peas), baigan bharta (mashed aubergine) or pindi channa (curried chickpeas). These may be served with rice, chapattis and chatni (pickle). Punjabi-style sweets, such as halwa (carrots cooked with butter, sugar, milk and spices), are also very popular and can be found in shops in most large cities in Britain. Sikhs living here also enjoy British foods.

Traditionally, Sikh people sit on the floor to share meals. Mealtimes are a welcome chance to relax with family and friends.

Purity

As well as being vegetarians, Sikhs are forbidden to smoke, drink alcohol or take drugs. They drink water, tea, soft drinks, fruit juice or lassi (yoghurt mixed with water), instead.

Childhood
and growing up

Traditionally, children are highly valued in Sikh communities. Today, 14 per cent of Sikh households have three or more young children, and one in four British Sikhs is under 16 years old.

Naming ceremony

The birth of a new baby is celebrated by a visit to the gurdwara for a special ceremony to name the child. After a prayer, the Guru Granth Sahib is opened at random. The first letter of the first paragraph on the left-hand page is read out, and this is used as the first letter of the baby's name. Many Sikh families like to choose names with a religious meaning, such as Gurmeet (Friend of the Guru) or Harbir (Warrior of God).

Young women sing hymns at their local gurdwara. Growing up as a Sikh means lots of community gatherings, lessons and activities alongside other Sikhs.

Some boys may go through a special ceremony between the ages of 11 and 16 years old. It is called 'Dastar Bandi', and is carried out in the presence of the Guru Granth Sahib, either in the gurdwara or at home. The boy's first turban is tied around his head by his maternal uncle. This is a Punjabi tradition.

WOMEN AS EQUALS

Boys and girls, and men and women are all treated equally in the Sikh religion. Guru Nanak, founder of the Sikh religion, taught that women were men's companions, and equal to them in all activities, from worship to war. He also valued women as educators, who brought up children to be good citizens and taught them Sikh spiritual values. He said: 'We are bound with the world through woman...Why should we talk ill of her...there is none without her.'

Schooling

In Britain, there are 64,000 Sikhs of school age. Most go to state-run schools. Some also attend classes in traditional Punjabi arts, music, dancing and the Sikh religion at their local gurdwara on Sundays. Young, British-born Sikhs are much more likely than their parents' generation to do well at school, and continue their education at college or university.

At school, some Sikh children wear western-style uniforms. But, for special occasions, most Sikh girls wear a traditional salwar kameez (a long tunic with trousers) in bright colours and beautiful fabrics.

Weddings and funerals

Most Sikhs believe that marriage is very important. Guru Nanak said that it joins 'two souls in one body'. Twice as many British Sikhs as white majority Britons live in married households, and Sikhs are less likely to be separated or divorced than any other Britons.

The bride and groom at this Sikh wedding hold each end of a pink silk scarf as a sign that they are joined together for life.

Marriage

Traditionally, Sikhs do not live together before marriage. Young British Sikhs also marry later than the national average, so they can complete their education or start their careers. Only 12 per cent marry before the age of 24.

Weddings

In the past, Sikh marriages were arranged by parents. But today, many young British Sikhs choose their own partners, although there are still some arranged marriages, and some disputes over them. Sikhs are tolerant of other religions, but only Sikhs may marry in the Anand Karaj (Ceremony of Bliss), held in a gurdwara or community hall. After prayers, hymns and speeches, the bride and groom bow low to the Guru Granth Sahib and walk around it four times, linked by a pink or orange scarf (the colours of life and joy). After more prayers, and a reading from the Guru Granth Sahib, everyone shares karah parshad.

At funerals a Granthi reads to the mourners from the Guru Granth Sahib.

Preparation

When a Sikh nears death, a Granthi (someone who looks after the Guru Granth Sahib) from the gurdwara may sit with them to read from the Guru Granth Sahib. Their friends and family may visit, to pray and offer holy gifts, such as morsels of specially-blessed food.

Funerals

After death, the body is respectfully washed, wrapped in clean white cloth and carried to its resting place while mourners sing hymns or say prayers. Elaborate displays of grief are discouraged, because Sikhs believe that people's spirits live on after death, and will be reborn. It is traditional for a Sikh to be cremated. While this takes place, there are more prayers, and readings from the Guru Granth Sahib.

MEMORIALS

Most Sikhs do not believe in putting up tombstones or other memorials, because the dead person's spirit is no longer connected to the 'empty' body that is left behind.

19

Focus on Birmingham

About 985,900 people live in Birmingham, in the West Midlands.

Industries

Until the late 20th century, Birmingham was famous for its jewellery, car-making and metal-working industries. Today, manufacturing is still important, but there is high unemployment. Sikhs, along with the rest of Birmingham's community, are affected by this.

A Sikh family walks down a street in the Handsworth district of Birmingham, one of Britain's busiest Sikh neighbourhoods.

Sikhs in Birmingham

Birmingham is home to many people of Asian, African and Caribbean decent. Together, they make up 29.6 per cent of Birmingham's citizens. The Sikh population numbers around 28,330 – 2.9 per cent of the city's total population. Most Sikhs live in five inner-city districts: Sandwell, Soho, Ladywood, Handsworth and Hall Green. Their homes are mostly terraced or semi-detached houses, built for 19th-century workers.

GURU NANAK NISHKAM SEWAK JATHA

The gurdwara on Soho Road, in Handsworth, was opened in 1977. It is one of the most spectacular buildings in Birmingham, with its marble-covered walls and traditional Sikh architecture. Open 24 hours a day, the Guru Granth Sahib is read continuously inside.

Community

There are around 40 gurdwaras in and around Birmingham, and many other organisations run by, and for, the Sikh community. These include cultural societies, social groups, political associations, youth clubs, women's groups, dance and music classes, Punjabi classes, welfare organisations and missionary societies. The Naujawan Academy is a group of Sikh volunteers who arrange holidays, sports and classes in music, arts and computing. They also run awareness seminars about problems such as drugs, bullying and racism, plus a confidential helpline. The Birmingham Sikh community also runs newspapers, radio stations broadcasting news and kirtans (religious songs), and Punjabi programmes on local television.

An elderly Sikh couple chat on a street in Birmingham. The city's Sikh community has become well-established in their lifetime.

"I strongly believe that it is important to have more Black and minority ethnic magistrates to ensure that the Bench is more representative and has a better understanding and awareness of cultural diversity. I feel that by becoming a magistrate, I can make a positive contribution and give something back to the community.

Ravinder Johal, magistrate.

Professionals

Sikhs in Birmingham are also active in schemes set up by national and local government to empower minority communities, and improve facilities for them. In 2004, Ravinder Johal became the first Asian woman to be appointed a magistrate (local judge). Sikh professionals also play an important part in many educational, health care and health promotion schemes.

Sikhs at work

Traditionally, Sikhs believe working hard is an important part of life and Sikhs in Britain have some of the highest levels of employment.

Jobs in Britain

Many jobs done by Sikhs are essential to the smooth running of Britain's economy. One in seven Sikh men and one in six Sikh women works in the transport and communications industries. Around 10 per cent of Sikh women work as factory operatives. Although Sikhs are one of the least likely groups in Britain to be professionals or managers, this may change as young British Sikhs become better educated.

Public service

Other Sikhs have chosen to devote themselves to public service careers. There are Sikh MPs and members of the House of Lords. In 2004, Sikh Lord Sucha Bains became Coventry's first Asian Lord Mayor. Darra Singh held a senior post at the Audit Commission (which monitors government spending) before becoming Chief Executive of Luton.

A Sikh optometrist (eyesight expert) tests the vision of a patient in his modern consulting room.

Sikh entrepreneurs

There are some spectacularly successful Sikh
entrepreneurs. Reuben Singh became Britain's youngest
self-made millionaire at the age of 22, after setting up a
chain of accessory shops while he was still at school. Tom
Singh founded New Look Plc, one of the UK's largest fashion retailers
in 1969. It now has over 500 stores. Jasminder Singh, who arrived in
Britain from Kenya in 1970, now owns many of Britain's most
prestigious hotels. In 2004, his business was valued at £350 million.

> Sikh businessmen and women run many small shops in Britain's cities. They often specialise in clothing and fabrics.

> **I work for the British Council and really enjoy it. A few other Sikhs work in my office and although we are allowed to, we choose not to wear traditional clothes into work. We prefer to wear western clothes like trouser suits. We change when we get home though!**
>
> *Sikh mother of 3, London.*

Entertainments, sports and festivals

British Sikhs have many religious festivals. Vaisakhi commemorates the day in 1699 when Guru Gobind Singh initiated the Khalsa. It is a time for music, dancing, new clothes and family parties. Some British Sikhs also like to listen to religious broadcasts from the Golden Temple at Amritsar, India, the Sikhs' holiest shrine.

Diwali

Diwali commemorates the founding of the city of Amritsar in 1577, and the day Guru Har Gobind freed 52 kings from prison. A late autumn festival, it also celebrates the power of light over darkness. Sikhs hold parties, light candles and arrange firework displays.

Sikhs carrying new orange flags, called Nishan Sahibs, march through the streets to celebrate the festival of Vaisakhi.

Gurpurb

Gurpurb festivals honour events in the Gurus' lives, such as birth, death or martyrdom. They are celebrated with an Akhand Path. This is a non-stop reading of the Guru Granth Sahib that takes 48 hours. It is followed by prayers and a celebration meal in the gurdwara.

This Sikh family is playing instruments traditionally used for religious music. From left to right, harmonium (keyboards), tabla (drums) and sitar (stringed instrument).

Music and films

For relaxation, many older Sikhs listen to classical Indian music or traditional Punjabi songs. Young Sikhs – like many other people in Britain – listen to Bhangra music, with its lively beat, played by artists such as Bally Sagoo, from Birmingham. Sikh DJs, such as Manchester's Tigerstyle, are also popular. People of all ages enjoy lavish Bollywood films made in India.

GURINDER CHADHA

Gurinder Chadha was born in Kenya but educated in the UK. She is now one of Britain's most successful film-makers. Her films, such as *Bahji on the Beach*, *Bend it Like Beckham* and *Bride and Prejudice*, combine British and Asian themes and are popular throughout the world.

A sitar has 19 strings. The player uses four strings for the tune, three to create the rhythm, and the other 12 to provide a backing drone (humming sound).

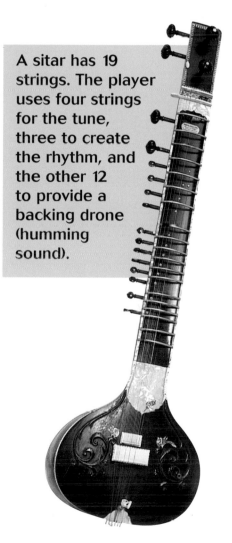

Sports

The most popular sports among Sikhs in Britain are cricket and hockey. Gatika (Sikh martial arts) champion Kamlajit Singh Aujila was recently named Asian Sports Personality of the Year, and represents Great Britain in international tournaments.

Threats and problems

Like other ethnic minorities in Britain, some Sikhs suffer from racist attacks. In a recent survey, 41 per cent of Asians said they believed Britain was a racist society, and 34 per cent said they had experienced racism at work.

Hostile environment

This hostility became much worse after 11 September 2001. Sikh men were attacked because of the way they looked, often being viewed as possible Muslim terrorists. New security measures, especially at airports, have made travel difficult for Khalsa Sikhs as they carry with them a kirpan at all times.

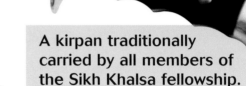

A kirpan traditionally carried by all members of the Sikh Khalsa fellowship.

A Sikh girl prays in her school uniform. Some young Sikhs find it hard to follow their faith in Britain.

Disadvantages

One disadvantage that Sikhs face in Britain is that many of the older members cannot speak English, which adds to the pressures of making a new life as an immigrant in Britain. Some young Sikh people find it hard to follow their faith, and fit in with other teenagers who choose free and easy lifestyles.

> "Many of us agree that Britain is a modern multiracial society, and welcome that. Yet, at the same time, we think racism is on the increase.
>
> *Gurbux Singh, Chairman of the Commission for Racial Equality, 2002.*"

The banner in this Sikh festival procession carries the message: 'Recognise all the human race as one' in English and Punjabi.

Punjabi

There are also religious tensions within the British Sikh community. Sikh worship takes place in the Punjabi language, but many young Sikhs, born in Britain, no longer speak it. They are calling for worship to be in English, but traditionally-minded Sikhs do not agree.

Calendar

Many Sikhs disagree about which calendar to use. The traditional Vikrami calendar slips behind the Western calendar by about 20 minutes each year. A new 'Nanakshahi' calendar, devised by a British-based Sikh, has tried to solve this problem. Introduced in 1999, it is now used by over 90 per cent of Sikhs worldwide. But a few Sikhs, in Britain and elsewhere, still do not accept it.

SAMOSAS AND OTHER SNACKS

Sikh medical staff are warning fellow-Sikhs to change their diet after finding that fatty Punjabi snacks, such as samosas (deep-fried pastries), are leading to a health crisis. In Birmingham, for example, Sikhs have one and a half times the level of heart disease and three times the level of diabetes compared to the city's white population.

Future hopes and fears

In a recent survey, 74 per cent of Sikhs living in Britain identified themselves as British. Over half also said that their faith was important to their identity. Most British Sikhs hope to continue living as good citizens. But many also hope to strengthen Sikh worship, values and lifestyle.

National council

In 2003, British Sikhs set up a new Sikh Federation and National Council of Gurdwaras. Both aim to raise awareness of Sikh people in Britain, and to link isolated Sikh communities so that they work together. These groups are not party political and do not plan to put forward candidates in national elections. Their aim is to lobby the main political parties with their concerns.

Recognition

These pressure groups' demands include greater representation for Sikhs in public bodies; improved funding for Sikh organisations; single-faith schools for Sikh children; preserving Sikh heritage and protecting Sikh human rights.

The Sikh tradition of Sewa (service to others) encourages men, women and children to be good neighbours.

<blockquote>
I think for too long Sikhs have been fairly quiet on issues that matter to them.

Dabinderjit Singh, of the Sikh Secretariat – an organisation that pushes for action on Sikh-related issues.
</blockquote>

Parliament

Already, Members of Parliament in London have promised support to British Sikhs. Sikhs are being trained as magistrates and the police and the army are keen to recruit Sikhs into their ranks. Recently, the army has eased uniform rules with regards to wearing a turban, and appointed a Sikh chaplain.

Britain's Sikh youth

Just as important, young Sikh people are asking Sikh elders to let them help run gurdwaras, and make decisions that will affect the next generation. They have called for an end to quarrels among Sikhs, and for 'vision and strategy' to plan the future. They have asked British Sikhs not to forget their faith and copy Western customs, but instead to create a proud and strong Sikh community.

These members of a Sikh family all look forward to a challenging new future for Britain's Sikh community.

Glossary

Bollywood the largest film industry in the world, based in Mumbai, India.

Chakkar part of the Sikh religious symbol. It represents the perfection of God, and also the universal brotherhood of Sikhs.

chapatti a thin, round bread used in Indian cooking.

entrepreneur someone who sets up and finances new, profitable businesses.

ethnic belonging to a group through descent or culture.

Golden Temple Sikhs' holiest shrine, in Amritsar, India.

Granthi the word Granthi comes from Granth (the Holy Scripture). A Granthi looks after the Guru Granth Sahib, and is always in attendance of it.

gurdwara a Sikh temple.

Guru a religious leader.

Guru Granth Sahib Sikh scriptures that are treated as the eleventh, and last, Guru.

immigrant somebody who has moved to a country to live permanently.

Indian subcontinent the region in southern Asia made up from the countries of Bangladesh, India, Pakistan and Sri Lanka.

karah parshad a mixture of wheat, sugar and butter, shared among worshippers as a sign of God's generosity.

Khalsa Panth a fellowship founded in 1699 by Guru Gobind Singh to unite Sikh believers and strengthen them in their faith.

meditate to empty the mind of thoughts or to think about something calmly, while relaxing.

merchant somebody who buys and sells goods.

multicultural the mixing of cultures of different countries, ethnic groups or religions.

Punjab an area divided between India and Pakistan.

Race Relations Act the Race Relations Act 1976, as amended by the Race Relations (Amendment) Act 2000. It makes it unlawful to discriminate against anyone on grounds of race, colour, nationality (including citizenship), or ethnic or national origin.

racist prejudiced towards people from certain races.

reincarnation the belief that a soul returns to live another life in a new body after death. It is also known as transmigration of the soul.

settler somebody who has moved to live in a new place.

shrine a place of worship.

topknot an arrangement of hair on top of the head.

turban a headdress worn by Sikh men that consists of a long piece of fabric wrapped around the head.

World War I a war fought between 1914 and 1918 in Europe.

Further information

This is a selection of websites that may be useful for finding out further information on Sikhism and Sikhs in Britain.

www.allaboutsikhs.com
> a site containing lots of useful information on Sikhism

http://atschool.eduweb.co.uk/carolrb/sikhism/ sikhism1.html
> A site for children about Sikhism

www.fairlands.herts.sch.uk/gurdwaratour/sikh _gurdwara.htm
> a virtual visit to a Sikh gurdwara

http://re-xs.ucsm.ac.uk/re/places
> a site containing lots of useful information on Sikhism

www.bbc.co.uk/religion/religions/sikhism
> a BBC site with useful links

www.bbc.co.uk/london/yourlondon/united colours/sikhism/welcome_history.shtml
> information about Sikhs in London

www.sikhnet.com/
> a site for Sikhs worldwide containing information, news and activities

www.sikhs.org.uk/default.asp?mnid= main&pgid=faq
> frequently asked questions about Sikhism

Note to parents and teachers

Every effort has been made by the Publishers to ensure that these websites are suitable for children, that they are of the highest educational value, and that they contain no inappropriate or offensive material. However, because of the nature of the Internet, it is impossible to guarantee that the contents of these sites will not be altered. We strongly advise that Internet access is supervised by a responsible adult.

Index